The Impact of Socialization on Personality Development

(Graduate essay, Kent State University, 1990.)

BY

David B. McCoy

The author would like to thank Mary Ann D'Aurelio who endures all
early drafts and offers sound editorial advice; Dr. Valerie J. Steffen
(primary advisory); Dr. Averil McClelland (Education advisory); Dean
Anderson; and Dr. Rhonda Baughman for proofreading the revised,
2014, draft.

Spare Change Press®
Massillon, OH 44646
sparechangepress79@gmail.com

INTRODUCTION

Social development is seemingly built upon a paradox (Damon, 1983). At the same time we are becoming social beings, we are also becoming individuals with distinct personalities. The reason why this dual process may appear paradoxical is because of the specialization that has taken place in the social sciences. Sociologists, over the years, have focused their attention on the socialization process through which a culture's rules of conduct are learned. Psychologists have, instead, focused on personality development, which is more concerned with the emergence of individual differences in behavior that make each person recognizably unique. Only of late has there been any real movement to join the two sciences in the realization that one aspect of the process cannot take place without the other, and that individual differences which constitute our distinctive personalities, in part, involve variations in the extent to which we conform to social norms (Damon, 1983; Hurrelmann, 1988; Zigler, Lamb and Child, 1982).

A definition of socialization that reflects this new view of social development is offered by Klaus Hurrelmann (1988): "Socialization....is the process of the emergence, formation, and development of the human personality in dependence on and in interaction with the human organism, on one hand, and the social and ecological living conditions that exist at a given time within the historical development of a society on the other" (P. 2). Those who use this definition of socialization accept the basic assumption that socially conveyed influences on personality development actually exist. This essay will explore how some personality traits are acquired by a person through the imparting of basic norms, values, and standards of behavior in a given society.

To avoid any misconceptions, I wish to present the parameters under which I worked.
This essay takes an interdisciplinary approach to the subject of socialization and personality development. The three branches of

knowledge utilized for this investigation include Sociology, Psychology, and Education.

The intent of this essay is not to propose possible changes in society toward sex equity. The sole intent is to gain an understanding as to how cultural norms (particularly sex roles) influence personality development.

Although this essay is confined to social influences on personality development, it is not the author's intent to imply that biological predispositions and cognition play no part in the process. Biological influences certainly must play some part in the development of certain personality traits, but as of yet, too many questions remain unanswered to make conclusive statements about that process. And because few people become mere reflections of their socializing agents, it is obvious that each of us has some cognitive control over his or her own development (Damon, 1983).

While this essay deals only with childhood or primary socialization, it again is not the author's intent to give the impression that socialization and personality development are static. Today it is widely accepted that socialization and resocialization take place throughout the adulthood, but that adult socialization is built upon aspects of primary socialization, which is the period essential in creating a person and in shaping the identity, outlook, skills, and resources of the evolving individual (Handel, 1988).

Several schools of thought dominate present day social and personality theory. A few of these include Psychoanalysis, Cognitive-Developmental, Behavior Genetics, Social Interaction, and Social-Cognitive Learning Theory. This essay uses as its general theoretical framework Social Interaction and Social-Cognitive Learning Theories.

SOCIALIZATION

Newborn homo sapiens are biological organisms with the predisposition to develop into social persons or what we call "human" (Berger and Luckman, 1967; Zigler, Lamb, and Child, 1982). Infants become human as they acquire the abilities to appreciate and use the symbols and embellishments brought into being by preceding generations (Koller and Ritchie, 1978). Becoming human includes learning to interact with others in appropriate ways; forming affectionate ties; participating as a member of various organizations; sharing loyalty with many unknown others who are fellow citizens; and internalizing the norms, values, roles, and patterns of behavior of the society to which one is born. Becoming human also includes development of the "self" or a personality. Personality may be defined as "the set of relatively stable and distinctive styles of thought, behavior, and emotional responses that characterizes a person's adaptations to surrounding circumstances" (Wortman and Loftus, 1985). The process by which one acquires these qualities, thus becoming human, is known as socialization.

Society intrudes itself into the socialization process in numerous ways. Society establishes the standards that socialized individuals are expected to achieve in physical development, in skills and capacities, in emotional expression, in intellective purposeful activities, and in the patterning of their relations with significant others (Inkeles, 1968). In their effort to socialize children, parents are guided by their awareness of such social expectations and by their image of what children must become if they are to live successfully in the world. Parents are also guided by their image of what makes "good parents" and most invest a great deal of time and effort living up to this standard (Clausen, 1968).

In modern societies where cultural traits have grown too numerous and complex for the family alone to transmit, institutions have been created. The primary institutions in our society include the family, the church, the educational system, the government, and the economic system, and each has been charged with the responsibility of transmitting a set of specific societal norms and values. Any violation of these intended norms or values is generally met with powerful sanctions. The mere allocation of sanctions constitutes a declaration of society's intent and sets a standard that will affect individuals regardless of whether they, themselves, receive the punishments or rewards of a given institution.

AGENTS OF SOCIALIZATION

Socialization is often divided into two broad stages, primary-childhood socialization and secondary-adult socialization. Considered the most important stage, primary socialization shapes the identities, outlooks, and resources upon which secondary socialization is built (Berger and Luckmann, 1967; Handel, 1988). Primary socialization is under the control of significant others. Significant others are those (parents, grandparents, siblings) who positively or negatively affect the life, personality, and orientation of children by exposing them to certain experiences, values, and roles, as well as restricting them from undesirable influences. Additional agents, or forces, of primary socialization include the public school system, peer group associations, and television.

The Family

As an institution, the family has been specifically assigned the responsibility of socializing children into competent, moral, and self-sufficient adults. Even when other institutions (i.e. schools, churches) have been granted "in loco parentis," ultimate authority and discretion in child-rearing still rests with parents (Gecas, 1981; Zigler et al., 1982).

By and large, parents are effective agents of socialization, and the roles, values, norms, and beliefs held by grown children are in congruence with the general socialization goals held by parents. Despite the fact much of the socialization is inadvertent, unintentional, and often unconscious on the part of parents, there are several reasons why parents remain highly effective agents. First, one or both parents generally spend a great deal of time with their children. Second, parents are powerful—they are bigger, stronger, and in control of the environment. Third, parents provide nurturance, but also dish out rewards and punishments. Fourth, parents control what and who their children will be exposed to. Finally, and probably most important, children strive to imitate their parents' behavior and obtain their approval (Mussen, 1967; Zigler et al., 1982). Contrary to general belief, parents remain highly influential in the socialization of their children well through adolescence, providing they remain accepting and available to their children (Adams and Gullotta, 1989; Clausen, 1968).

For children to achieve the performance requirements of a given society, parents must, to some degree, fulfill the following responsibilities or tasks: 1) Providing of nurturance, affection and warmth that should permit children to develop a sense of trust and incentive to model the parents' behavior. 2) Training aimed at the appropriate expression of basic biological impulses, such as toilet training and giving up breast or bottle feeding for solid foods. 3) Teaching, skill-training, and opportunities for practice of basic motor skills (crawling, walking), language and cognitive skills, and self-care skills. 4) Orienting children to their immediate world of kin, community, and society in a variety of social situations and settings. This would include explaining the dangers and behavioral requirements of those social situations. 5) Transmitting cultural goals and values, and motivating children to internalize these as their own. 6) Promoting interpersonal skills as well as modes of feeling and behaving toward others. 7) Controlling the scope of their childrens' behavior, limiting transgressions, correcting errors, and providing guidance—all the while helping children formulate personal goals and feelings of autonomy (Clausen, 1968).

The Public School System

Due to the size and complexity of the cultural base of most developed nations, societies have created public schools. The public school, like the family, is an institution whose explicit mandate is to socialize children. Unlike the family, though, the school's mission is more narrow and more formal in scope (Gecas, 1981). What's more, schools build upon the foundations of personal qualities laid down by the family (Koller and Ritchie, 1978).

A generally accepted list of "official" socialization tasks of the public school system include: 1) Teaching of basic cognitive skills such as reading, writing, arithmetic, and the more general skills of maintaining attention, sitting still, and participating in classroom activities. 2) Helping children develop skills in abstract thinking and problem solving. 3) Transmitting the cultural heritage from which children may develop an appreciation of their society and its past. 4) Transmitting dominant cultural goals and values, making clear their meaning and relevance. 5) Teaching vocational skills that will help children enter the job market—but not so much in terms of training for specific occupations as in identifying and equipping children to be able to absorb special skills and necessary knowledge. 6) Training children to become citizens for life within the political system. 7) Preparing children to live among and form meaningful relationships with other people. 8) Teaching the special aspects of culture, such as art, music, literature, drama, science, technology, and sports (Clausen, 1968; Koller and Ritchie, 1978; Thomas and Anderson, 1982).

In addition to the most obvious socialization goals of public schools, there are objectives that are not so obvious (and like within the family, these may not be obvious even to teachers). These objectives often fall under the heading of the "hidden curriculum" and include the following tasks for the student: 1) Becoming acquainted with and accepting of uniform standards of treatment and evaluation as opposed to the special, personal treatment operating in the family. 2) Learning to relate more to people in role-specific ways, which are more temporary, interchangeable, and impersonal than family roles. This also includes learning that relative strangers wield considerable power and that power is often unequally held by men and women. 3) Learning independence and responsibility for one's own actions, as well as learning to be self-motivated. 4) Learning to live in crowded, urban situations. This includes learning to wait in lines (i.e. recess, lunch, dismissal), learning to wait for people (i.e. slower students to complete a task, the teacher's attention), and learning to wait for supplies and resources (scissors, books, the drinking fountain, the pencil sharpener). 5) Learning to adapt to the continued and pervasive spirit of evaluation that becomes official, public, and dominant during the school years (Gecas, 1981; Jackson, 1988).

Upon closer examination, it becomes evident that for children to make their way satisfactorily through the school system, they must master the tasks of both the "official" and "hidden" curricula. But it is ironic that the tasks that probably have the greatest importance in functioning as a member of society are on the latter list. In addition to the intended socialization goals mentioned above, another important function of public schools is to provide a transitional bridge between the family and the larger society.

Peer Group Associations

Like schools, peer groups become more influential as the influence of parents begin to wane. Peers supplement the influences of parents, schools, and the media by providing additional pressure toward conformity with conventional norms and standards, and tend to rely heavily on stereotypes to shape appropriate behavior (Zigler et al., 1982). In both experimental and naturalistic students, it has been found that children as young as three years of age reinforce and punish one another for sex appropriate and sex inappropriate behavior. Today, because of the increasing number of children enrolled in group-care facilities, peer group influences are probably being exerted sooner and may become increasing influential.

What is distinct about socialization in peer groups is the effect it has in social development (Fine, 1988; Gecas, 1981). First, peers provide staging areas for the exploration of role-taking, role negotiation, and self-presentation skills in a variety of ways (i.e. play, games, and group interactions). Through multiple peer group associations, in addition to the family and the school, children gain an understanding that they are capable of a repertoire of behaviors and roles, and that the most successful children are those who are able to remain flexible in projecting an appropriate self-image in a particular setting.

Second, peer groups provide settings for the experimentation and performance of behaviors that would otherwise be considered improper. This includes the performance of pranks (which allow children to explore allowable boundaries of behavior and to gain social poise in stressful situations), and a means of expressing sexual attitudes, aggression, frustration, and attitudes toward parents and school.

Third, peer groups are vital in transmitting information avoided by adults. This includes the practice of sex, how to "work the system", the art of negative evaluations (insults), and how to have excitement and adventure.

Perhaps the only intended goal of peer socialization is the relationship itself. Certainly, peers are aware of the power fellow group members have on behavior, but it is doubtful they have any real cognizance of the processes taking place (Clausen, 1968).

Television

Over the last four decades, a new and powerful agent of socialization has taken its place along side the other important influences on primary socialization—television. Shortly after its introduction in the early 1950s, television was viewed simply as a harmless form of entertainment, but it was gradually realized that television could have a powerful effect on a child's behavior. Particularly through the work of Albert Bandura, it was shown observational learning, or imitation, takes place regardless of whether the viewer is rewarded (Zigler et al., 1982). (This does not mean children will actually perform the learned behavior, but they will always have the capacity, once the behavior is learned).

Another concern was due to the fact that children watch a great deal of television. Most children are exposed to television by their first birthday and by age three have favorite programs. Preschoolers watch up to 2 ½ hours of television a day with a jump to 4 hours a day occurring around age eight. By the time children are eighteen years old, they will have spent as much time, if not more, watching television as in school (Honig, 1983; Liefer, 1974).

The greatest attention has been paid to three areas in which television influences socialization: Anti-social or aggressive behavior, pro-social behavior, and sex role development (the latter will be dealt with in the second portion of this paper).

What has become generally accepted by those investigating the impact of television on children is that, "A youngster's social development can be affected by continued exposure to certain kinds of media programming. These effects are not merely transient but can have a long lasting, malevolent influence on personality development" (Eron & Huesmann, 1987: 195). The malevolent influence television can have has been confirmed in two major studies. Stein and Friedrich (1975) exposed children between the ages of 3.8 and 5.5 to three types of television programs: violent cartoons ("Batman" and "Superman"); neutral children's programs; and pro-social programs (Mr. Rogers' Neighborhood"). Their study confirmed that viewing aggressive programs increased aggressive behavior, decreased self-regulation (children showed a decline in tolerance of delay and in rule acceptance), and disrupted interpersonal interactions between peers (where children were less cooperative and relied more on aggression in frustrating peer interactions). Children who saw neutral programs showed more aggression than those children who saw pro-social programs—results of viewing pro-social programs will be discussed shortly.

A second study by Jerome and Dorothy Singers and Wanda Rapaczynski (1983) also found a relationship between viewing violent programs and aggressive behavior in children. In addition to their finding, they found certain variables useful in predicting future aggression in children. These variables include: 1) Heavy viewing of violent programs. 2) Children granted unrestricted viewing (programs and hours of viewing time). 3) Homes where there is an emphasis on physical discipline. The reason why television has such an impact is because it gives children more opportunities for modeling aggressive behavior, and children viewing violent behavior on television come to believe the recurring aggressive behavior is socially sanctioned. An interesting contradiction in their overall findings was that some children who actually watched less television became more aggressive than those children who watched more television. It was found these children watched less television, but watched more violent, adult programs.

During the early 1960s, an experiment performed by Feshbach stood in contrast to most findings on television and aggressive behavior. Feshbach found that a viewer's aggressive energies were drained off or released through the vicarious experience of viewing someone else's aggression. This "catharsis" hypothesis has been tested numerous times, but experiments generally reject the notion (Leifer, 1974; U.S. Department of Health and Human Services, 1982).

What has been confirmed, though, is that children learn not only negative behaviors from television, but they also learn pro-social, positive behaviors. In their study, Stein and Friedrich also found that those children shown the pro-social program, "Mr. Rogers' Neighborhood," increased in task persistence, rule acceptance, and tolerance of delay. Coates, Pusser, and Goodman (1976), with the intent of extending the work by Stein and Friedrich, compared the impact of watching "Sesame Street" (which is primarily concerned with the development of cognitive skills) and "Mr. Rogers'" (which is primarily concerned with stressing individual uniqueness and self-worth). Coates found that those children watching "Sesame Street" increased in social contacts, in giving positive reinforcements, but also in inflicting punishments. On the other hand, children watching "Mr. Rogers'" increased in social contacts and in giving positive reinforcements, but there was no increase in inflicting punishments.

Based on the research in this area, several things can be concluded concerning the impact of television viewing on primary socialization: 1) Whether anti-social or pro-social television programs, the more frequently children rehearse behaviors by continued viewing, the more likely those behaviors will be remembered and reenacted. 2) By consistently observing either anti-social or pro-social behaviors, children come to believe that what they are viewing represents appropriate ways of behaving. 3) Parents can, by controlling what their children watch, have a great impact on their children's behavior.

MECHANISMS OF SOCIALIZATION

One major distinction between primary and secondary socialization is that children during primary socialization (birth through age twelve) form images of the roles and attitudes of significant others, and may even play at some of those roles, but it is during secondary socialization that individuals acquire role-specific knowledge and vocabularies actually rooted in social institutions (Berger and Luckmann, 1967). Another major difference between the two periods is that secondary socialization is more self-initiated role taking, where primary socialization proceeds more through observational learning, elementary forms of role taking (i.e. games and play), and social reinforcements (Bush and Simmons, 1981; Mead, 1969).

Observational Learning

Children acquire many of their stable patterns of social behavior, outlooks and strategies through the observation of social models (Aronfreed, 1969; Wortman and Loftus, 1985). Social models and influences during primary socialization consist mainly of those agents previously discussed. From observing others, children form ideas of how new behaviors are performed, and on later occasions this information serves as a guide for action (Bandura, 1977). In general, children have "the capacity to program a rather high-fidelity replication of the exact topography of a model's behavior," and their "imitation often emerges with remarkable suddenness and accuracy, after only very limited exposure to a model" (Aronfreed, 1969: 282).

In the scheme of social learning, modeling influences serve at least five functions according to Albert Bendura (1986): 1) They teach component skills and provide rules for organizing them into new structures of behavior. 2) They strengthen or weaken inhibitions over behavior that has been previously learned. 3) They serve as social prompts for previously learned behavior that observers can perform but have not done because of insufficient inducements. 4) They not only draw observers' attention to particular objects or environmental settings, but extend children's perceived use of objects or settings (i.e. children may learn that a mallet can be used not only to pound pegs, but to pummel a doll or other children). 5) Lastly, they can elicit emotional arousal in children when seen in others.

As the leading proponent of this theory, Bandura (1977, 1986) has identified four component processes that govern observational learning: Attentional processes—the exploration and perception of modeled activities; retention processes—the conversion of experiences into symbolic representations; production processes—the organization of learning subskills into new response patterns; and motivational processes—the acquisition of intention to use or not use observationally acquired competencies.

Attentional Processes

Children cannot learn from observation unless they attend to relevant aspects of modeled behavior. Attentional processes determine what is selectively observed from ongoing modeled events and consists of several identifiable determinants. First, people with whom children regularly associate, particularly if they are significant others and they are nurturant, are more likely to be attended to. Second, new or highly conspicuous (salient) behavior is readily perceived over ordinary behavior. Third, attention is heightened when the performance produces observable, rewarding or punishing outcomes for models. Also, children will be more likely to select models who are proficient at producing good outcomes than models who generate negative outcomes.

Retention Processes

Children cannot be influenced to any great extent by the observation of modeled behavior unless they form a symbolic representation of a behavior in their memory. Observation learning relies mainly upon two representational systems—imaginal and verbal. Sensory stimulation gives rise to perceptions (images) of the external events, and through repeated exposure, modeled stimuli eventually produce enduring, retrievable images of modeled behavior. Visual memory plays a predominate role in observational learning during the early periods of primary socialization when verbal skills are lacking. Even after verbal skills have been fully developed, visual imagery continues to play a vital role in learning behaviors that do not lend itself readily to verbal coding (i.e. information about spatial and temporal coordinations).

The second representational system, which accounts for the notable speed and retention of observed behavior, involves verbal coding. In fact, most of the cognitive processes that regulate behavior are largely verbal rather than imaginal in nature. "Because of the extraordinary flexibility of verbal symbols, the intricacies and complexities of behavior can be conveniently captured in words" (Bandura, 1986: 58).

Children who code modeled behavior into either words, labels, or vivid imagery retain that behavior better than children who simply observe or are mentally preoccupied with other matters while watching models. In addition to initial representation, verbal and visual coding are of little use if they are forgotten. To ensure that observed behavior is not lost, it must be mentally rehearsed or actually performed. The highest level of observational learning is achieved by first organizing and rehearsing a modeled behavior symbolically and then enacting the behavior overtly.

Production Processes

The next component of modeling involves converting symbolic representations into action. In the initial phase of the production process, desired responses are selected and organized at the cognitive level. The newly formed conceptions of action then enable children to produce at least a rough approximation of a modeled behavior. Because behavior and ideas are rarely transformed into correct actions without error on first attempts, accurate matches are usually achieved through corrective adjustments of the initial efforts. Discrepancies between the symbolic representation and the actual execution serve as one cue for needed corrective action. Another guide to accurate performance comes from onlookers in the form of corrective verbal information, praise, or punishment.

Motivational Processes

Despite having observed and symbolically represented modeled behavior, children do not enact everything they learn. Performance of learned behavior is governed by three sources of incentives—direct, vicarious, and self-produced. When a performance is followed by a rewarding, external outcome there is an increased chance the behavior will be repeated. On the other hand, if the external outcome is unrewarding or punishing, then the likelihood the behavior will be repeated declines. Observed (vicarious) outcomes influence performance in much the same way as direct incentives—behavior that has rewarding consequences for a model is favored over behavior that has negative consequences. Also, personal standards of conduct provide a further source of motivation. Children express behavior they find self-satisfying and reject what they personally dislike.

While numerous factors govern observational learning, modeling of desired behavior occurs best when models demonstrate a desired behavior repeatedly, instruct observers to follow the behavior, prompt observers verbally and physically when they fail, and reward observers when they succeed. Failure to model a desired behavior results when observers do not attend to relevant behavior, inadequately model behavior in symbolic form, fail to rehearse a behavior, or there exists insufficient incentives to bring about a behavior.

Role Taking

Although people are born members of a society, it is the roles they play (son-daughter, mother-father, student-teacher, employer-employee, male-female, etc.) that connect them to that society. While roles not only connect individuals to a society, they are sources of personal identities.

Nearly every role found in a given society is socially created and has its own specific "script" or set of norms according to which individuals are to act in a given position or situation. As long as individuals play their various roles as provided for in "scripts," the "social play" can proceed as planned. What is noteworthy about role playing and role taking is that we tend to absorb the norms and identities of our roles. This absorption is important to society because it allows people to be somewhat predictable in the ways they behave (Forisha, 1978) and assures that society will have the persons it needs to function (Berger, 1963). Consequently, roles are sources of motivation, values, norms, behaviors, emotions, attitudes, and perhaps most important, roles engender relatively stable concepts of reality (Berger, 1963; Gecas, 1982; Nisbet, 1970).

Generally, the learning of social roles is associated with adult or secondary socialization, but role taking actually develops very early in the socialization process—shortly after the acquisition of language and the ability of children to form symbolic representations (Baldwin, 1986; Mead, 1969). Prior to this time, infants simply copy the behavior of significant persons in their environment with no conception of differing roles (Anderson, 1988). The reason why language acquisition is so important to the process is that by hearing themselves talk, children gain a perception of their behavior and existence, which is separate from others in their environment. Once children have begun to use language and have some sense of self, role taking progresses in the form of play and games.

Much of childhood play is organized around social themes: playing at being something (mother, father, doctor, lawyer, nurse, policeman, fireman). When children play the roles of others, although they may focus only on fragments of roles, children still acquire some of the interests and characteristics of the roles. "While playing house, children take the roles of mother and father, thereby acquiring aspects of their parents' interests and selves;" or "If a little girl likes her kindergarten teacher and frequently role-plays being such a teacher, she may acquire some the interests and characteristics of her teacher" (Baldwin, 1986: 110; 97). It is through playing many different roles that children gradually acquire their own unique combination of personality traits.

Much of the information on playing the roles of others is gained through direct instruction and/or observation (Boudreau, 1986). Agents particularly important in defining roles for children include the family, television, peers, day care, and literature read to children. While much of the information provided is factual, a good deal of the information is based on stereotypic notions of what constitute appropriate role behavior. Stereotypes are a cluster of beliefs and attitudes used to categorize groups of individuals without regard for individual differences (Boudreau, 1986). Stereotypes include attributes considered characteristic of persons occupying particular roles, and may even imply who should or can best fill certain roles (Berger, 1963; Eagly, 1987).

It should be emphasized that children's role playing is much simpler than the role taking of adults. But even from simple forms of role playing children learn what roles exist in the society, what the expectations are for different roles, and which roles might be available to them as adults. It is also the period when children begin to actively place themselves in the appropriate gender role as established for by the society (Gecas, 1981). (This latter point will be an important focus in the next section of this essay.)

By the time they enter school, children have cognitively matured to where they can participate in games. Play is different from games in that play is a cooperative interaction that has no stated goal, rules, or winners. Games, on the other hand, are competitive interactions with formal norms (rules), specific players (roles), predetermined end-points, and winners (Lever, 1988).

Before reaching the game phase, children have no definite character or personality (Baldwin, 1986). However, as children play an established game, they learn to synchronize their behavior with the larger group and to respond to the rules of the game. Playing a game also requires children to know how all the other players will respond at any given moment. Put another way, children must take the attitudes and perspectives of everyone involved in the game, and realize that the different roles of the game have a relationship with each other.

Because games help children think in terms of the team or organized community, referred to by George Herbert Mead as the "generalized other," children increasingly see themselves as the whole group sees them, which in turn helps children move closer to a unified personality. Ultimately, once children can relate to the "generalized other" of games, they gain broadened and increasingly abstract perceptions of their "self," and are able to conceive of the "generalized other" in terms of broader social institutions (Mead, 1969).

Social Reinforcements

To ensure that children perform desired social behaviors (whether instrumental or learned), agents of socialization utilize social reinforcements. Social reinforcements can be defined as the actions of one individual to maintain, modify, or inhibit the behavior of another individual (Horowitz, 1967). Social reinforcements are vital because children rarely perform desired behaviors exactly the first few attempts. Therefore, social reinforcements serve to inform and guide children toward a desired performance. Social reinforcements also serve an important role in encouraging children to perform previously learned behaviors, as well as inhibiting the performance of undesirable behaviors. What can be stated in very general terms about social reinforcements is that behaviors positively rewarded are likely to be repeated and behaviors that are punished are likely to be inhibited or discarded.

In more specific terms, several points can be made about the characteristics of effective social reinforcements (paraphrased from Aronfreed, 1969; Bandura, 1986; Domjan & Burkhard, 1986;

Maccoby, 1968; McCandless, 1969; Parke, 1970, 1974). First, both rewards and punishments are necessary for effective results. When both rewards and punishments are administered, children learn not only what they can do but also what they cannot do. But more learning does seem to occur when the balance is tipped in favor of rewards or positive reinforcements. Second, rewards and punishments are more effective if they are delivered immediately after the response to be established or inhibited. The problem for children when there are long delays is they may associate reinforcements with other responses made during the delay completely unrelated to desired or undesired responses. One way to off-set this problem is to symbolically (through verbal means) reinstate the nature of desired or deviant acts and then deliver reinforcements. Third, reinforcements administered consistently are more effective than reinforcements that are not. When reinforcements are not consistent, it is difficult for children to form associations between behavior and reinforcements. Fourth, for reinforcements to have any effect, children must have a positive nurturing attachment to the reinforcing agent. Particularly with punishment, it appears that a nurturant punishing agent arouses greater anxiety in children than does a neutral agent because such a high value is attached to the behavior of the nurturant agent. In a study carried out by Sears (cited in Parke, 1970), it was found that mothers rated warm and affectionate found spanking an effective means of discipline, but mothers who were rated cold and hostile reported spanking ineffective. Fifth, for punishment to be very effective, it must be used in conjunction with rationale. Not only must the reason for the punishment be explained, children must be offered alternative ways of behaving that will bring forth rewards as opposed to punishments. Sixth, a complete reliance on strong verbal or physical punishment will not be enough to bring about a total internalization (the adoption of social norms and roles by children without external stimuli) of desired behaviors. The adoption of norms and roles seem to be brought about most effectively through the withdrawal of affection by nurtural agents.

Withdrawal of affection includes such forms of punishment as ignoring or isolating children, rejection, and coldness. Reinstatement of affection is dependent upon an agreement to behave in an appropriate manner. The believed reason why withdrawal of affection is so powerful is that when punishment becomes too aversely abusive, anxiety levels reach such heights that feelings of anxiety cannot become independent of the external punishment. The punishment then becomes the main focus of attention. Instead, through omission of rewarding stimuli, children are encouraged to focus on their behavior, and to draw their own conclusions about acceptable means of reducing anxiety, shame, or guilt. But three points need to be made about the use of withdrawal of affection:

For withdrawal of affection to be effective, a nurturant relationship must exist between a parent (or agent) and a child.

The nurturant agent must be sure the child knows what behavior was unacceptable and inform the child what behavior will reinstate the lost rewarding stimuli.

Prolonged withdrawal by the nurturant person may drive the child to seek an undesirable reliance on peers for social approval.

A final characteristic about social reinforcements is that children need not directly experience stimuli. The effects of rewarding or punishing reinforcements can be experienced vicariously. Seeing the actions of others produce good (bad) results increases (decreases) the likelihood that observers will behave in similar or related ways.

SEX ROLE SOCIALIZATION

"By far the most complex, difficult, and all-pervasive role a person learns to play is that of 'male' or 'female'" (Brannon, 1985: 301). A sex role is defined as a set of behavioral and personality characteristics expected of a person solely on the basis of gender. And while the American culture assumes our sex roles, which parallel our divisions of labor, are based on innate, biological qualities, many scholars reject that notion. They repeatedly point to the wide variation of sex roles found in different cultures and to the inception of our own sex roles in the last 300 years (Brannon, 1985: Deaux, 1987; Lyon, 1986; M. Mead, 1969; O'Kelly, 1986; Romer, 1981; Toffler, 1980; Wilson & Boudreau, 1986). The idea that sex roles are biological is also rejected by social learning theorists and social interactionists alike. Albert Bandura (1986) writes: "Although biological characteristics form a basis for gender differentiation, many social roles that get tied to gender are not ordained by biological differences. Gender-role development is, therefore, largely a psychosocial phenomenon" (p. 92). The social interactionist, Spencer Cahill (1983) notes: "...anatomical and biological differences between individuals, including those related to chromosomal sex, are not intrinsically meaningful....biological differences between the sexes do not directly influence sex-role development. The effect is indirect, a result of typical social reactions to such differences" (p. 2).

The process of acquiring behaviors, attitudes, skills, and standards assigned on the basis of one's gender is known as sex role socialization. The focus of this portion of the essay, based on existing evidence, will be to examine the socialization process of sex role development, and to show that differing male-female personalities are in part due to boys and girls being worlds apart in the way they are socialized.

Sex role development is a viable means of understanding the socialization process because the development of sex-typed behaviors occurs under the same principles invoked in other areas of socialization (Mischel, 1970). Furthermore, parents in all socioeconomic, educational, and cultural groups tend to have the same ideas about sex related expectations for children (Block, 1981).

The Family and Gender Identity

The first step in sex role acquisition is for children to develop their own gender identity. To help parents and other people organize their view of boys and girls, societies have created male-female categories which include information directly related to such male-female features as anatomy, reproduction functions, divisions of labor, and personality attributes (Bem, 1987; Romer, 1981). Closely tied to each category are labels and stereotypes that aid in coding and sorting information (Mischel, 1970). Because these responses are sexually differential, children soon learn which attributes and labels are linked with their own sex category, and, hence, with themselves (Bem, 1987; Cahill, 1983; Cowan and Hoffman, 1986).

Beginning from the birth of their children, parents respond differently to boys than to girls. Rubin, Provenzano, and Luria (1974) found that parents perceived male infants to be different from female infants in personalities and behavior within twenty-four hours of birth. Parents of girls reported their babies to be softer, smaller, and less attentive than did parents of boys—even when doctors reported no significant differences. Parents do not realize they view boys and girls differently; they simply think they are responding appropriately with the stimulation their children prefer (Zigler et al., 1982).

Armed with the cultural beliefs that females are nurturant, passive, and dependent, and males are active, aggressive, and assertive, parents form expectations as to their children's behavior. It has been shown that parents respond more warmly and affectionately to girls, while boys are treated in a more aggressive and assertive manner (Boudreau, 1986). Boys, who are touched and held less than girls after 6 months of age, are played with more vigorously, are rewarded for rough and mischievous activities, and are given more freedom to explore. As they grow older, boys are also strongly discouraged from being "sissies," and are verbally instructed and sanctioned from straying too far from sex-typical behavior. Girls, who are generally more restricted and supervised in their behavior by parents, are expected to be sweet and docile, are discouraged from rough and mischievous behavior, and are talked to more frequently (Langlois and Downs, 1980; MacDonald and Parke, 1986; Chafetz, 1983; Whicker and Kronenfeld, 1986).

Not only do parents perceive and interpret boys' behavior differently from that of girls, parents create vastly different physical environments that increase the likelihood of sex-typical behavior. Parents dress female babies in pink with bows and frills; boys are dressed in blue or some sort of a sports outfit. Parents also give infants sex-appropriate toys and furnish their rooms accordingly. Girls' rooms contain dolls, stuffed animals, housekeeping toys such as rolling pins, dishes, and stoves, floral decorations, and ruffles— which encourage imitation and emphasize home maintenance and nurturing activities. Boys' rooms contain educational materials, clocks, sports equipment, toy or real animals, cars and trucks, and military toys—which encourage inventiveness and manipulation (Block, 1981; Romer, 1981; Russo, 1985). Consequently, the sex-typed play materials children are given channel their spontaneous play into traditionally feminine or masculine roles (Bandura, 1986).

Children learn a great deal about sex roles by observing their parents' performance of household tasks. While the general notion is that fathers pick up some of the slack as wives enter or return to the work force, by and large this is not the case. In numerous studies cited by Matlin (1987), fathers' role in the performance of household tasks increase very little. In fact, husband and wives tend to hold firm to traditional attitudes about their "proper" roles in family life (Lein and Blehar, 1983; Scanzoni, 1983). One area where fathers have made noticeable strides is in the care of children. Perhaps this will present a less stereotypic view of fathers to children, but due to the evidence that fathers treat sons and daughters differently, one must conclude the more active fathers become in parenting, the greater the differences that will develop between boys and girls (Hoffman, 1988).

Sex role stereotypes, labels, sex-typed toys and environments, and parents' performance of household tasks all constitute important dimensions with which children come to interpret, organize, and make sense of the social environment, as well as how they perceive themselves (Macklin and Koble, 1984; Schwartz and Markham, 1985). The impact of parent behavior can be observed in that fact that sex role stereotypes, labels and preferences for sex-appropriate toys are reliably observed in children as young as 26 months of age (Leinbach and Fagot, 1986; Weinraub, Clemens, Sockloof, Ethridge, Gracely and Myers, 1984; Urberg, 1982). By 31 months of age, most children can place themselves in the proper sex category and they actively seek to confirm their gender identity by adopting appropriate behaviors, attitudes, and preferences (Lewis and Weinraub, 1979; Reis and Wright, 1982). As children move closer to sex constancy (the understanding that gender remains constant despite superficial changes in such things as clothing, toys, games, etc.) around the age of five, males and females behave differently because they have come to perceive, evaluate, and regulate both their own behavior and the behavior of others in accordance with cultural definitions of gender appropriateness and their emerging sense of self (Bem, 1987; Boudreau, 1986).

Peers

A second important agent in sex role development is the peer group. By age three, not only do most children know and actively seek to conform to the rules regarding sex appropriate behavior and attitudes, they actively pressure their peers to conform to conventional sex-typed norms and standards (Zigler et al., 1982; Lamb, Easterbrooks, and Holden, 1980).

Besides encouraging appropriate sex-typed behavior, peers encourage segregation of the sexes into same-sex groups (Matlin, 1987). This may be due to a number of reasons. First, once children are able to categorize themselves on the basis of sex, they are attracted to that category with its stereotypical behavior—preferring to focus on information that confirms their sex category (Mischel, 1970; Boudreau, 1986). Second, as noted above, peers are quite willing to punish members of their sex who stray too far from appropriate behavior. Third, parents structure their children's environment to provide "appropriate" male-male/female-female contacts (see Feiring and Lewis, 1987). Fourth, while this split is partly due to boys actively seeking to conform to sex role stereotypes and appropriate behavior, and fear of punishment for inappropriate cross-sex behavior, there emerges a struggle for power between boys and girls. Girls, who mature earlier than boys in social skills, take early control of mixed-sex groups; boys are welcome only if they play passive baby or father roles. Boys, socialized to be assertive and aggressive, by age four find they are inhibited from taking power in mixed-sex groups because girls will ignore or withdraw from aggressive acts, or female adult models will step in to stop boys from causing harm. Therefore, to fulfill their expected assertive and aggressive behavior, boys form their own same-sex groups. Consequently, as boys fully explore limits of aggressive behavior and struggle for power within their all-male groups, they quickly develop skills in negotiating control and formulating strategies for competition (Pitcher and Schultz, 1983).

Janet Lever (1988), in her observations of the varying complexity of children's games, also found sex differences in the development of social skills. Lever measured the complexity of play and games along six dimensions: role differentiation (how many distinct roles occurred in the game), player interdependence (whether the action of one player affected the performance of another), size of the play group, explicitness of goals, number and specificity of rules, and team formation. Her study revealed the following:

1) In role differentiation, the largest category of girls' public activities were the same as their private activities, namely, single-role, turn-taking play. Each player, in specified order, attempted to accomplish the same task as all other players. Boys by age 10-11

have largely stopped playing central-person games for team sports with multiple roles (team captains, subordinates, and playing positions).

2) In player interdependence, very little was required of girls engaging in single-role, turn-taking play—coaction rather than interaction was required. It may be true turn-taking holds elements of competition between individual members, but what was seen was each player acting independently of the others; competition was more against a figurative "scoreboard." When boys competed as individuals, they were more likely to engage in face-to-face confrontations, or to compete as members of teams where they had to simultaneously coordinate their activities with those of their teammates, while taking into account the actions and strategies of their opponents.

3) In size of play groups, boys played in much larger groups than did girls. Boys typically were involved in team sports requiring 10-25 or more persons; girls typically played in groups of two or three participants, seldom larger than 5 or 6.

4) In explicitness of goals, games played by girls were loosely structured, cooperative, conversational, governed more by ritual than rules, and played only until players were bored. Boys, who granted much more importance to structure, rules, and competition, placed great importance on being proclaimed the winner.

5) In the number and specificity of rules, girls' games were primarily turn-taking in nature, players progressed in identical order, and because competition was primarily against the "scoreboard," rules were few and simple. But where games were competitions between individuals or teams, as with boys' games, there was great need for broad sets of elaborate rules covering a wide variety of situations in order to prevent ambiguities. Thus, it might be said that girls "played" more while boys "gamed" more.

6) Because of the dual-structured relationship of cooperation (with teammates) and conflict (against the opponents) of boys' games, team formation was seen as an added dimension of complexity. Girls, as noted, seldom engaged in team play.

Due to differences in nature and complexity of boys' and girls' play and games, boys and girls acquire different social skills. Boys acquired such skills as coping with impersonal rules, working for collective as well as personal goals, and dealing with competition in a forthright manner. Girls, instead, acquired affective and verbal skills. Childhood games certainly teach boys and girls different abilities and identities, but just as girls may not learn to be rational, competitive, and rule-oriented, boys may not learn to be nurturing and emotionally expressive (Anderson, 1988 on Lever).

Television

In addition to having direct role models to observe and imitate in their parents, children are also exposed to the stereotyped world of television. In both cartoons and television programs, traditional masculine and feminine stereotypes are portrayed (Mackin and Kolbe, 1984; Whicker and Kronenfeld, 1986). But in contrast to findings concerning the relation of children's behavior and their viewing of aggressive or prosocial television programs, Kevin Durkin (1985a,b,c) contends that there has been no strong or convincing relationship established between the amount of viewing stereotyped television programs and an impact on sex role beliefs or attitudes.

According to Durkin, the myth that such an association exists is due to three widely cited studies with which he finds major limitations. The first is the Beuf study of 1974. This study is shown to "provide few quantitative data, no statistical support, and suffers from other limitations in method" (Durkin, 1985a: 196). The two other studies carried out by McGhee and Frueh (Frueh and McGhee, 1975; McGhee and Frueh, 1980) are found to contradict one another, and "the (1975) study and the (1980) study produced mutually incongruous results...which lead the investigators themselves to a revised position, now minimizing observational learning from television as an explanation of sex role stereotyping in children" (Durkin, 1985a: 63).

Besides rejecting the three widely cited studies, Durkin presents three other studies, which failed to show any correlation between viewing and sex role beliefs and attitudes. These studies by Cheles-Miller (1975), Meyer (1980), and Perloff (1977) are important because they used considerably larger numbers of subjects, and although each of these studies failed to find the expected correlation between viewing and stereotyping, each showed effects related to domestic factors such as maternal employment and maternal attitudes.

One study on the effects of heavy viewing of television that supports and refutes Durkin's position is that by Michael Morgan (1982). In his two-year study of 349, 6th through 10th graders, he found that for girls, a heavy amount of television viewing predicted increased scores on an index of sex role stereotyping for one year; but no significant link between how much television watched by boys and what they thought one year later was found. Morgan's explanation for such discrepancies may be due to the "mainstream phenomenon." Under this notion, heavy viewing on the part of girls brings them in line with similar "mainstream" views already held by boys and society as a whole.

One area that has shown positive correlations between television viewing and sex role stereotyping is in counter-stereotyped programs, which have had some success in reducing stereotyped beliefs. In a study of approximately 7,000, nine-to-twelve-year-old children, Johnston and Ettema (1982) [cited by Durkin, 1985c] succeeded in bringing about limited changes in the acceptance of girls engaging in athletic, mechanical, leadership, and independent roles; acceptance of boys engaging in nurturing activities; and acceptance of woman and men in non-traditional careers. But such desired changes in attitude occurred only when the 13-part, counter-stereotyped program (Freestyle) was shown in school and followed by a post-program discussion. If children viewed the program at home, or at school with no post-program discussion, few attitude changes occurred. And despite changes in attitude of the viewing/discussion groups, children maintained traditional beliefs concerning the male primary breadwinner role.

This seems to indicate children have limits on how far they are prepared to tolerate modifications and reversals of sex roles.

While the full impact of television on sex role development and sex role stereotyping in children is not known, it is known that as children near gender constancy they are more likely to pay attention to same-sex models (Bussey and Bandura, 1984; Ruble, Balaban and Cooper, 1981). Such behavior indicates children may use television to supplement, reinforce, and complement other sources of information they have about male and female social roles.

Schools

The last agent of sex role development to be examined is the educational system, which plays a significant part in emphasizing, reinforcing, and expanding differences that exist in children when they enter school (Block, 1983; Boudreau, 1986).

In the recent past, schools took an active role in socializing boys for future provider-occupational roles and girls for nurturant-family roles. Present-day public schools are generally prohibited by law from providing different services and treatment to boys and girls, but subtle inequalities remain (Lockheed, 1985). The differences in treatment of boys and girls fall under the description of the "hidden" curriculum. "The 'hidden' curriculum is a term used to refer to those aspects of learning in schools that are unofficial or unintentional, or undeclared consequences of the way in which teachers organize and execute teaching and learning" (Davies and Meighan, quoted in Lobban, 1978: 52). It is believed by many the "hidden" curriculum is more influential in shaping pupils' attitudes than the "official" curriculum, particularly since sex differences first observed in early elementary school become more pronounced with the number of years children spend in school (Benz, Pfeiffer and Newman 1981; Boudreau, 1986). To understand the forces at work, two facets of the "hidden" curriculum will be examined: student-teacher interactions and authority structures.

On average, girls enter school better equipped than boys to play the role of student, which stresses the norms of politeness, cleanliness, and obedience, and frowns on vulgar language and fighting (Levine and Ornstein, 1981). But such preparedness may, in fact, function to make girls less visible, inhibit their learning process, and lead to differences in self-expectancies for success (Boudreau, 1986). Conversely the competitive, self asserted, and non-conforming behavior of boys may create greater adjustment problems, and may lead boys toward greater independence, autonomy, and higher self-esteem (Levy, 1973).

One possible explanation is there are observable, sex-based differences in student-teacher interactions. In research by David and Myra Sadker (1986a,b), teachers talked more to boys, questioned boys more, gave boys more precise (praise, criticism, and remediation) responses, gave boys detailed instructions for performing tasks, and allowed more opportunities for boys to respond (answer questions, give opinions, help out). Girls received more general and personal instructions, criticisms and questions, had tasks done for them, and engaged in fewer precise interactions with teachers.

Teachers also criticized boys and girls for different things. Boys are praised for their good academic work and punished for disruptive behavior. In contrast, girls are rewarded for good behavior and criticized for poor or sloppy academic work. Thus, when boys fail to meet academic standards, teachers tend to attribute their failure to misbehavior. When girls fail to meet academic standards, because girls generally conform to classroom rules, teachers tend to attribute their failure to low academic ability (Boudreau, 1986; Lobban, 1978).

The way in which disruptive behavior is dealt with by teachers also differs for boys and girls—boys, generally are scolded and criticized more harshly than are girls. At first glance, it would appear such unequal treatment would have a negative effect on boys, but the reverse is true. Boys soon learn they can get attention from teachers and respect from male peers (who encourage conventional male sex stereotypes) for misbehavior. At the same time they learn how to deal with criticism and to defend and assert themselves. When equal criticism is denied girls, it may lead to anxiety, oversensitivity to criticism, and a tendency to do tasks to gain social (adult) approval rather than to meet one's own needs and standards (Block, 1983; Levy, 1973). To compound this problem, the Sadkers (1986a) discovered boys are eight times more likely to call out and demand attention than girls. Surprisingly though, when boys call out, teachers tend to accept their answers, but when girls call out, teacher remediate their behavior and advise them to raise their hands. Such unequal treatment teaches boys to be assertive and teaches girls their answers and ideas are not valued and they should remain passive.

Student-teacher interactions are not limited to verbal exchanges; the "hidden" curriculum can be transmitted through nonverbal communication as well. In examining patterns of touching behavior between preschool teachers and children, Perdue and Connor (1978) identified four types of touches: "Friendly" (touches that occurred as an expression of nurturance or approval), "Helpful" (touches that occurred while a teacher was helping a child), "attentional" (touches intended to focus or control behavior), and "incidental" (touches that were accidental). Their study revealed that when male teachers touched girls, the touch was more likely to be a "helpful" touch; but when male teachers touched boys there was a tendency for the touch to be of a "friendly" nature. No significant differences in the relative frequency with which female teachers gave "friendly," "helpful," "attentional," or "incidental" touches to boys and girls were found. These findings lead Perdue and Connor to conclude, "Differences in nonverbal communication to boys and girls may serve as an additional source of information about the sex roles they are expected to assume" (p. 1261).

Marianne LaFrance (1985), in her review of Perdue and Connor, offered an explanation as to why subtle verbal and nonverbal student-teacher interactions are so powerful in maintaining and expanding sex role differences and why these interactions are so difficult to overcome. First, nonverbal and subtle verbal cues are the primary avenues through which people receive evaluative messages. Verbal praise and criticism provide students with information about what they are doing, but nonverbal and subtle messages convey to pupils much about who they are. Second, subtle nonverbal processes may be especially important for understanding interactions where children are involved due to limited vocabularies. Third, subtle interaction messages are less under conscious control and hence less subject to self-monitoring and accountability.

In addition to unequal student-teacher interactions, schools themselves reinforce sex differences and traditional roles in the authority structure (Block, 1981). Males hold more prestigious positions, like principalships and supervisory jobs, and while females make up more than 80% of the teaching force, fewer than a quarter of the principals are women (Sadker, 1986b). If "observation of extrafamilial roles also help children to learn about sex differences in social power...[and] children imitate in varying degree the behavior of many of these models" (Mischel, 1970: 29, 31), then we might indeed wonder whether the implicit message that pupils get from our male-dominated educational system is that power and maleness are associated with one another, and femaleness is associated with the subservient role (Lobban, 1978)? In testing the possible influence of real-life male and female models on children's perception of the position of school principal, Paradise and Wall (1986) found children with male principals were more likely to indicate that more men can be principals; and children with female principals indicated that either men or women can be principals. Thus, "the presence of a principal of a particular sex appears to have exercised considerable influence over children's perceptions" (Paradise and Wall, 1986: 6).

CONCLUSION

The intent of this essay was to explore how aspects of personality are acquired through socialization. While biological and cognitive factors may play a part in personality development, society intrudes itself onto the process by the way in which it sets standards of behavior, establishes values, prescribes appropriate ways of interacting, and determines the numerous roles needed for the society to function. It was shown that important mechanisms of socialization include observational learning, role taking, and social reinforcements. Agents during primary socialization include the family, schools, peers, and television. In order to understand how socialization can influence personality development, sex role socialization was investigated. Sex role socialization provides a viable way of understanding the process because it involves the same principles invoked in other areas of socialization. While this essay brought forth no new knowledge to the subject, it is hoped the interdisciplinary approach might bring a broader understanding of the impact of socialization on personality development.

REFERENCES

Adams, G. and Gullotta, T. Adolescent Life Experiences. Pacific Grove: Brook/Cole, 1989.

Anderson, M. Thinking About Women. New York: Macmillian, 1988.

Aronfreed, J. "The concept of internalization." In D. Goslin (Ed.), Handbook of Socialization Theory and Research. Chicago: Rand McNally, 1969.

Baldwin, J. George Herbert Mead. Newbury Park: Sage, 1986.

Bandura, A. Social Foundations of Thought and Action. Englewood Cliffs: Prentice-Hall, 1986.

Bandura, A. Social Learning Theory. Englewood Cliffs: Prentice-Hall, 1977.

Berger, P. Invitation to Sociology: A Humanistic Perspective. Garden City: Anchor, 1963.

Berger, P. and Luckman, T. The Social Construction of Reality. Garden City: Archor, 1967.

Bem, S. "Masculinity and femininity exist only in the mind of the perceiver. " In J. Reinisch, L. Rosenblum, & S. Sanders (Eds.), Masculinity/Femininity. New York: Oxford, 1987.

Benz, C., Pfeiffer, I., and Newman, I. "Sex role expectations of classroom teachers, grade 1-12." American Educational Research Journal, 1981, 18, 289-302.

Block, J. "The differences between boys and girls: How gender roles are shaped." Principal, 1981, 60, 41-45.

Block, J. "Differential premises arising from differential socialization on the sexes: Some Conjectures." Child Development, 1983, 54, 1335-1354.

Boudreau, F. "Sex roles, identity, and socialization." In F. Boudreau, R. Sennott, & M. Wilson (Eds.), Sex Roles and Social Patterns. New York: Praeger, 1986.

Brannon, R. "Dimensions of the male sex role in America." In A. Sargent (Ed.), Beyond Sex Roles. St. Paul: West Publishing, 1985.

Bush, D. and Simmons, R. "Socialization processes over the life course." In M. Rosenbery and R. Turner (Eds.), Social Psychology. New York: Basic Books, 1981.

Bussey, K. and Bandura, A. "Influences of gender constancy and social power in sex-linked modeling." Journal of Personality and Social Psychology, 1984, 47, 1292-1302.

Cahill, S. "Reexamining the acquisition of sex roles: A social interactionist approach." Sex Roles, 1983, 9, 1-15.

Chafetz, J. "Society determines sex roles." In B. Leone & M. O'neil (Eds.), Male/Female roles. St. Paul: Greenhaven Press, 1983.

Clausen, J. (Ed.). Socialization and Society. Boston: Little Brown, 1968.

Coates, B. Pusser, H., & Goodman, I. "The influence of 'Sesame Street' and 'Mister Rogers' Neighborhood' on children's social behavior in the preschool." Child Development, 1976, 47, 138-144.

Cowan, G., & Hoffman, C. "Gender stereotyping in young children: Evidence to support a concept-learning approach." Sex Roles, 1986, 14, 211-224.

Damon W. Social and Personality Development. New York: Norton, 1983.

Deaux, K. "Psychological constructions of masculinity and femininity." In J. Reinisch, L. Rosenblum, & S. Sanders (Eds.), Masculinity/Femininity. New York: Oxford, 1987.

Domjan, M. and Burkhard, B. The Principles of Learning and Behavior. Pacific Grove: Brooks/Cole, 1986.

Durkin, K. "Television and sex role acquisition. 2: Effects." British Journal of Social Psychology, 1985a, 24, 191-210.

Durkin, K. "Television and sex-role acquisition: 3: Counter-stereotyping." British Journal of Social Psychology, 1985b, 24, 211-222.

Durkin, K. Television, Sex Roles, and Children. Milton Keynes: Open University, 1985c.

Eagly, A. Sex Differences in Social Behavior: A Social-Role Interpretation. Hillsdale: Lawrence, 1987.

Eron, L. and Huesmann, R. "Television as a source of maltreatment of children." School Psychology Review, 1987, 16, 195-202.

Feiring, C., & Lewis M. "The child's social network: Sex differences from three to six years." Sex Roles, 1987, 17, 621-636.

Fine, G. "Friends, impression management, and preadolescent behavior." In G. Handle (Ed.), Childhood Socialization. New York: Aldine De Gruyter, 1988.

Forisha-Kovach, B. Sex Roles and Personal Awareness. Morristown: General Learning Press, 1978.

Gecas, V. "Contexts of socialization." In M. Rosenberg and R. Turner (Ed.), Social Psychology. New York: Basic Books, 1981.

Handel, G. Childhood Socialization. New York: Aldine De Gruyter, 1988.

Hoffman, L. "Changes in family roles, socialization, and sex differences." In G. Handel (Ed.), Childhood Socialization, New York: Aldine De Gruyter, 1988.

Honig, A. "Research in review. Television and young children." Young Children, 1983, 38, 63-75.

Horowitz, F. "Social reinforcement effects on child behavior." In W. Hartup and N. Smothergill (Eds.) The Young Child. Washington, D.C.: National Association for Education of Young Children, 1967.

Hurrelmann, K. Social Structure and Personality Development. New York: Cambridge, 1988.

Inkeles, A. "Society, social structure, and child socialization." In J. Clausen (Ed.), Socialization and Society. Boston: Little Brown, 1968.

Jackson, P. "The daily grind." In G. Handel (Ed.), Childhood Socialization. New York: Aldin DeGruyter, 1988.

Koller, M. and Ritchie O. Sociology of Childhood. Englewood Cliffs: Prentice-Hall, 1978.

LaFrance, M. "The school of Hard Knocks: Nonverbal sexism in the classroom." Theory Into Practice, 1985, 24, 40-44.

Lamb, M., Esterbrooks, M., & Holden, G. "Reinforcement and punishment among preschoolers: Characteristics, effects, and correlates." Child Development, 1980, 51, 1230-1236.

Langlois, J., & Downs, A. "Mothers, fathers, and peers as socialization agents of sex-typed play behavior in young children." Child Development, 1980, 51, 1237-1247.

Leifer, D., Gordon, N., and Graves, S. "Children's television more than mere entertainment." Harvard Educational Review, 1974, 44, 213-245.

Lein, L. and Blehar, M. "Working couples as parents." In A.S. Sknolnick and J.H. Sknolnick (Eds.) Family in Transition. Boston: Little Brown and Co., 1983.

Leinbach, M., and Fagot, B. "Acquisition of gender labels: A test for toddlers." Sex Roles, 1986, 15, 655-666.

Lever, J. "Sex differences in the complexity of children's play and games." In G. Handel (Ed.), Childhood Socialization. New York: Aldine DeGruyter, 1988.

Levine, D. and Ornstein, A. "Education, socialization, and sex." The High School Journal, 1981, 64, 337-341.

Levy, B. "Sex role socialization in schools." In Sex Role Stereotyping in the Schools. Washington, DC: NEA, 1973.

Lewis M., Weinruab, M. "Origins of early sex-role development." Sex Roles, 1979, 5, 135-153.

Linn, M., and Peterson A. "Facts and assumptions about the nature of sex differences. In S. Klein (Ed.), Handbook for Achieving Sex Equity through Education. Baltimore: Johns Hopkins, 1985.

Lobban, G. "The influences of the school on sex-role stereotyping." In J. Chetwynd and O Hartneet (Eds.), The Sex Role System, London: Routledge and Kegan Paul, 1978.

Lockheed, M. "Women, girls, and computers: A first look at the evidence." Sex Roles, 1985, 13, 115-122.

Lyon, E. "The economics of gender." In F. Boudreau, R. Sennott, & M. Wilson (Eds.) Sex Roles and Social Patterns. New York: Praeger, 1986.

Maccoby, E. "The development of moral values and behavior in childhood." In J. Clausen (Ed.), Socialization and Society. Boston: Little Brown, 1968.

Macoby, E. and Jacklin, C. "Sex differences in aggression: A rejoinder and reprise." Child Development, 51, 1980, 964-980.

MacDonald, K., & Parke, R. "Parent-child physical play: The effects of sex and age of children and parents." Sex Roles, 1986, 15, 367, 378.

Macklin, M., & Kolbe, R. "Sex role stereotyping in children's advertising: Current and past trends." Journal of Advertising, 1984, 13, 34-42.

Matlin, E. The Psychology of Women. New York: Holt, Rinehart and Winston, 1987.

McCandless, B. "Childhood socialization." In D. Goslin (Ed.) Handbook of Socialization Theory and Research. Chicago: Rand McNally, 1969.

Mead, G. "Self." In A. Strauss (Ed.), George Herbert Mead On Social Psychology. Chicago: University of Chicago Press, 1969.

Mead, M. Sex and Temperament in Three Primitive Societies. New York: Dell, 1969.

Mischel, W. "Sex-typing and socialization." In P.H. Mussen (Ed.), Carmichael's Manual of Child Psychology, Vol. 2. New York: Wiley, 1970.

Morgan, M. "Television and adolescents' sex role stereotypes: A longitudinal study." Journal of Personality and Social Psychology, 1982, 43, 947-955.

Myers, D. Social Psychology. New York: McGraw-Hill, 1987.

Mussen, P. "Early socialization: Learning and identification." In T. Newcomb (Ed.), New Directions in Psychology III. New York: Holt, Rinehart and Winston, 1967.

Nisbet, R. The Social Bond. New York: Knoph, 1970.

O'Kelly, C. "The nature versus nurture debate." In F. Boudreau, R. Sennott, & M. Wilson (Eds.), Sex Roles and Social Patters. New York: Praeger, 1986.

Paradise, L., and Wall, S. "Children's perceptions of male and female principals and teachers." Sex Roles, 1986, 14, 1-7.

Parke, R. "The role of punishment in the socialization process." In R. Hoppe, G. Milton, and E. Simmel (Eds.), Early Experiences and The Processes of Socialization. New York: Academic, 1970.

Parke, R. "Rules, roles and resistance to deviation: Recent advances in punishment, discipline, and self-control." In A. Pick (Ed.), <u>Minnesota Symposia On Child Psychology</u>. St. Paul: Minnesota Press, 1974.

Perdue, V., and Connor, J. "Patterns of touching between preschool children and male and female teacher." <u>Child Development</u>, 1978, 49, 1258-1262.

Pitcher, E., & Schultz, L. <u>Boys and Girls at Play</u>. New York: Praeger, 1983.

Reis, H., & Wright, S. "Knowledge of sex-role stereotypes in children aged 3 to 5." <u>Sex Roles</u>, 1982, 8, 1049-1056.

Romer, N. <u>The Sex Role Cycle</u>. Old Westbury: The Feminist Press, 1981.

Roopnarine, J. "Mothers' and fathers' behavior toward the toy play of their infant sons and daughters." <u>Sex Roles</u>, 1986, 14, 59-68.

Rubin, J., Provenzane, F., & Luria, Z. "The eye of the beholder: Parents' view on sex of newborns." <u>American Journal of Orthopsychiatry</u>, 1974, 44, 512-519.

Ruble, D., Balaban, T., & J. Cooper. Gender constancy and the effects of sex typed televised toy commercials. <u>Child Development</u>, 1981, 52, 667-673.

Russo, N. "Sex-role stereotyping, socialization, and sexism." In A. Sargent (Ed.), <u>Beyond Sex Roles</u>. St. Paul: West Publishing, 1985.

Sadker, M., and Sadker, D. "Sexism in the classroom: From grade school to graduate school." <u>Phi Delta Kappan</u>, 1986a, 67, 512, 515.

Sadker, M. and Sadker, D., & Klein S. "Abolishing misperceptions about sex equity in education." <u>Theory Into Practice</u>, 1986b, 25, 219-226.

Scanzoni, J. <u>Shaping Tomorrow's Family</u>. Beverly Hills: Sage, 1983.

Schwartz, L., & Markham, W. "Sex stereotyping in children's toy advertisements." <u>Sex Roles</u>, 1985, 12, 157-170.

Scott, K. "Learning sex-equitable social skills." Theory Into Practice, 1986, 25, 243-249.

Singer, J. Singer, D., and Rapaczynski, W. "Family patters and television viewing as predictors of children's beliefs and aggression." Journal of Communication, 1984, 34, 73-89.

Stein, A., and Friedrich, K. "The effects of television on young children." In A. Pick (Ed.), Minnesota Symposia On Child Psychology, Vol. 9. Minneapolis: The University of Minnesota Press, 1975.

Thomas, W. and Anderson, R. Sociology. New York: Harcourth Brace Jovanovich, 1982.

Toffler, A. The Third Wave. New York: Bantom, 1980.

Urberg, K. "The development of the concepts of masculinity and femininity in young children." Sex Roles, 1982, 8, 659-668.

U.S. Department of Health and Human Services. Television and Behavior, Vol 1. Rockville: National Institute of Mental Health, 1982.

Weinraub, M., Clemens, L., Sockloff, A., Ethridge, T., Gracely, E., & Myers, B. "The development of sex role stereotypes in the third year: Relationships to gender labeling, gender identity, sex-typed toy preference, and family characteristics." Child Development, 1984, 55, 1493-1503.

Wilson, M., & Boudreau, F. "The sociological perspective." In F. Boudreau, R. Sennott, & M. Wilson (Eds.), Sex Roles and Social Patterns. New York: Praeger, 1986.

Whicker, M., & Kronenfeld, J. Sex Role Changes. New York: Praeger, 1986.

Wortman, C., Loftus, E., and Marchall, M. Psychology. New York: A.A. Knoph, 1985.

Zigler, E., Lamb, M., & Child, I. <u>Socialization and Personality Development</u>.
New York: Oxford, 1982.

www.ingramcontent.com/pod-product-compliance
Lightning Source LLC
Chambersburg PA
CBHW070258290326
41930CB00041B/2648